I'm Reading About

The GATEWAY ARCH

by Carole Marsh

Printed and Manufactured in Peachtree City, GA., USA www.gallopade.com

Book design: Susan Van Denhende

Editor: Janice Baker

Photo Credits: Cover: Semmick Photo/Bigstock.com. Pages 3&5: photo.ua/Bigstock.com. Page 8: Alfred Waud, The Historic New Orleans Collection. Page 13: Lewis and Clark National Historic Trail 2015.png by Geographyguy CC BY-SA 4.0. Page 14: Charles M. Russell, Amon Carter Museum of American Art. Page 17A: joeygil/Bigstock.com; 17B: afliegs/Bigstock.com. Page 18A: Jefferson National Expansion Memorial Archives; 18B: Collection Manuscripts & Archives, Yale University. Page 20: Missouri State Archives. Page 22: Gateway Arch by Shobi Ram CC BY-SA 3.0. Page 24: Sgt. Justin D. Pyle, U.S. Air Force. Page 26A: Gateway Arch tram car.jpg by Robert Lawton CC BY-SA 2.5; 26B: STL JNEM north tram base jpg. by Daniel Schwen CC BY-SA 4.0. Page 28: JNEM Observation deck.jpg by Daniel Schwen CC BY-SA 4.0; Gateway Arch windows.jpg by Kelly CC BY-SA 2.0. Page 30: rudi1976/Bigstock.com. Page 32A: Jefferson National Expansion Memorial by Gabriel Jorby CC BY-ND 2.0; 32B: AG-PHOTOS/Bigstock.com; 32C: GatewayArch-St.Louis-Missouri by Sam Valadi CC BY-SA 2.0. Page 34: povilac/Bigstock.com

The Gateway Arch is a great place to visit!

What is so special about the Gateway Arch?

Let's read about it and see!

INTRODUCTION

The Gateway Arch is a tall steel arch. It is the tallest man-made monument in the United States!

The Gateway Arch is a monument to Americans moving west to settle the United States. That movement is known as "westward expansion."

A monument is a structure built to remember a person or event.

Gateway Arch

LOCATION

The Gateway Arch is located in St. Louis, Missouri.
It is also called the "St. Louis Arch."
St. Louis was known as the "gateway" to the West!

The arch sits on the west bank of the Mississippi River.
St. Louis was where many settlers
started their journey west.

Some settlers traveled on land.
Some settlers traveled on rivers.

St. Louis,
Missouri
Mississippi River
Here it is!

HISTORY

What is "westward expansion"?
Westward expansion describes how Americans moved from east to west to settle the country.

Early colonists lived along the Atlantic coast. As America's population grew, people wanted new land for farming and hunting. Many people migrated westward. They moved over the Appalachian Mountains and beyond!

Moving West

HISTORY

In 1803, President Thomas Jefferson bought a huge amount of land from France. It was known as the "Louisiana Purchase."

The land stretched from the Mississippi River in the east to the Rocky Mountains in the west, and from the Gulf of Mexico in the south to Canada in the north.

The Louisiana Purchase doubled the size of the United States!

Louisiana Purchase

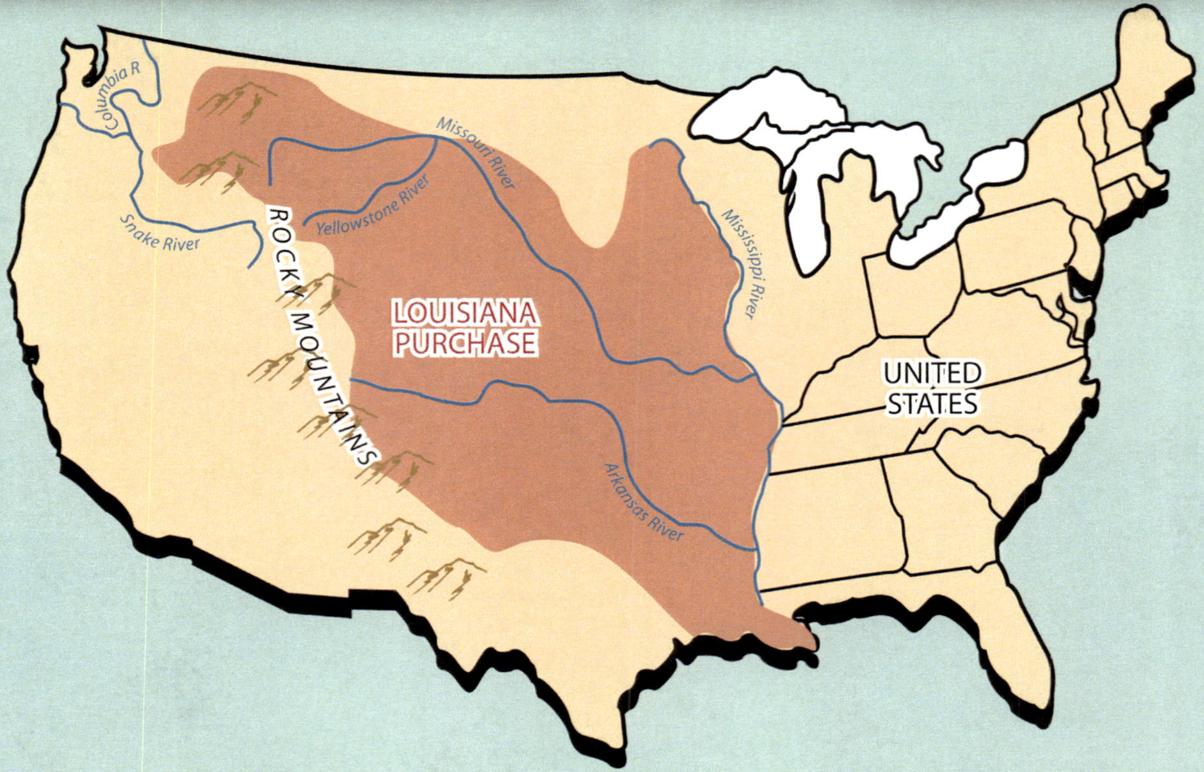

HISTORY

President Jefferson hired two men
to explore the new land:
William Clark and Meriwether Lewis.
The two men gathered supplies, men, and boats.
Captain Lewis even brought along his dog Seaman!

The Lewis and Clark Expedition started
where the Mississippi River meets the Missouri River.
That spot was just north of St. Louis, Missouri.

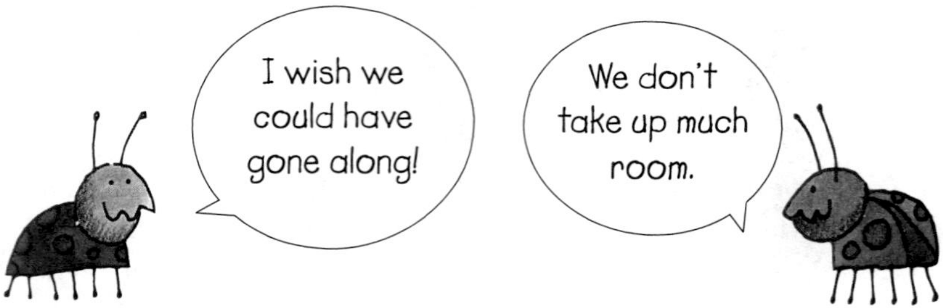

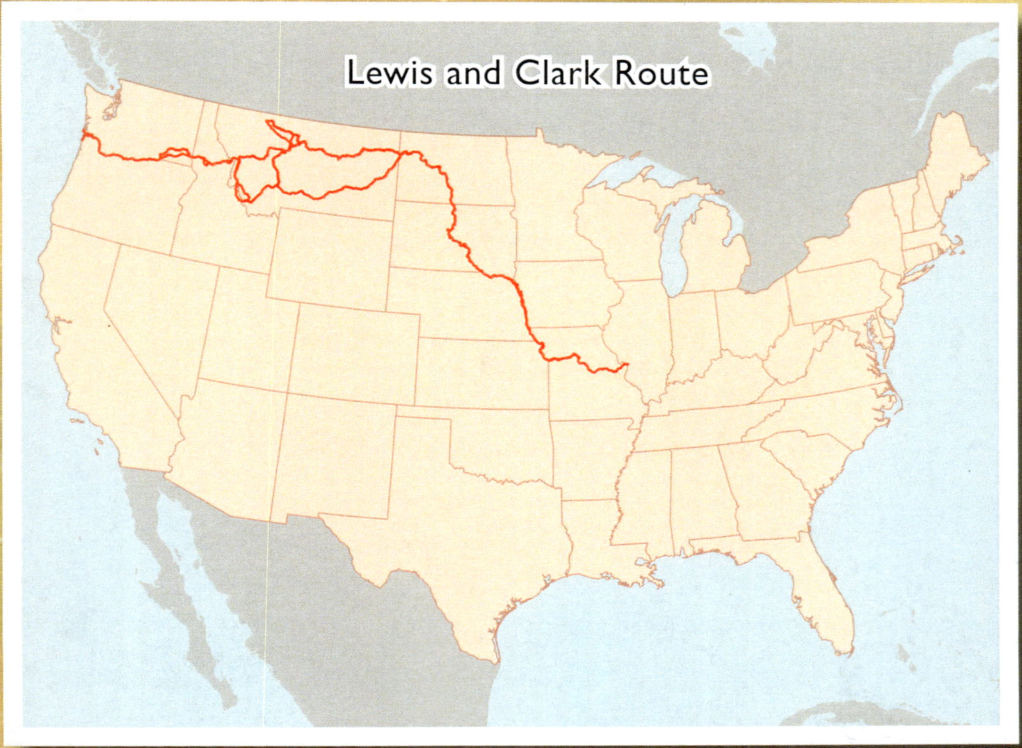

Lewis and Clark

HISTORY

It took Lewis and Clark two years to go to the Pacific Ocean and back. They traveled about 8,000 miles by boat, canoe, and horseback!

- They crossed raging rivers.
- They climbed huge mountains.
- They met new Indian tribes.

Lewis and Clark opened up the West for settlement!

Incredible Journey

MEMORIAL

The Jefferson National Expansion Memorial was created to help us remember how America was settled.

This memorial park honors the wise president and the brave explorers who helped America grow!

The Jefferson National Expansion Memorial includes the Gateway Arch and the Old Courthouse.

In 2017, a new Museum of Westward Expansion opened under the arch.

Jefferson National Expansion Memorial

Creative Contest

Eero Saarinen

Who had the idea for the Gateway Arch?

In 1947, a contest was held to design a special monument at the Jefferson National Expansion Memorial. It needed to represent the "gateway to the West." People were excited to see who would win!

An architect named Eero Saarinen won the contest. Saarinen was born in Finland. He moved to America when he was 13 years old.

CONTEST

Construction

Workers began to build the arch on February 12, 1963. It was an exciting time!

The construction company built a tower where people could watch the progress. In the first year, one million people watched the arch grow taller and taller!

The Gateway Arch was completed in October 1965.

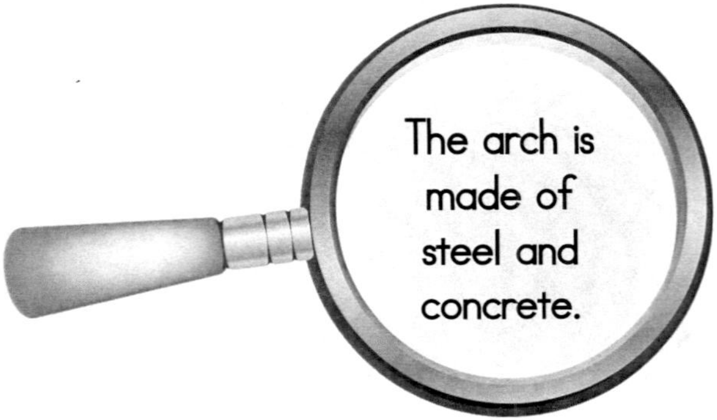

Strong and Stable

The legs of the Gateway Arch
go very deep into the ground.
That makes the arch very stable.

The arch can withstand high winds
and earthquakes.
It sways in high winds—
but not very much!

It takes winds of 50 miles per hour
to make the arch sway about an inch!

Awesome Arch

How tall is the Gateway Arch?
It is REALLY tall!

The Gateway Arch is
630 feet tall and 630 feet wide.
Its legs are 54 feet wide at the base.
It is the world's tallest arch!

The arch is tall.
The arch is wide.
Keep on reading
to learn what's inside!

Tram to the Top

TRAMS

Did you know you can ride
up to the top of the arch?

Inside the arch, there is a tram system with small cars.
The cars are also called "capsules" or "pods."
Each capsule holds five people.

The capsules glide up to the top of the arch.
It only takes about four minutes to get to the top!

Observation Deck

AT THE TOP

When you get to the top of the arch,
WOW! What a view!

You can look out windows on each side.
You can see the Mississippi River flowing below.
You can see the historic city of St. Louis.
On a clear day, you can see for 30 miles!

Each leg of the arch has a stairway.
Only arch workers can use the stairs.

Safe from Lightning

CRACK! BOOM!
I am a lightning bolt!
I may hit the Gateway Arch from time to time.
But there is nothing to worry about!

The arch has lightning rods at the top.
The rods help carry my electric current
safely to the ground.
That way, I can't do any damage!

Amazing
Arch

DID YOU KNOW?

Read these fascinating facts about the Gateway Arch!

- It cost $13 million to build.
- There are 1,076 steps in each stairway leg.
- The tram runs about 340 feet per minute.
- The arch is made of 142 stainless steel sections.
- The arch is the tallest monument in the Western Hemisphere!

MISSOURI
1821
CORPS OF DISCOVERY
1804
2004
2003
E PLURIBUS UNUM
National Historic
Landmark